Major,
    Thank you for supporting me and my first book. Remember that you can CONQUER anything!

        ♡

Conqueror

Conqueror

A Black Woman's Guide to Conquering Challenges in the Workplace

PAIGE BROWN

Table of Contents

About this Book

This book contains recollections of my experiences, particularly those in the workplace, as told from my perspective alone. While all the stories are true, some names and identifying details have been changed. I use these memories as fuel for advice to young women of color in the workplace, especially those who are pursuing a career in a STEM (Science, Technology, Engineering, or Math) field where they may be underrepresented.

As an African American and woman in engineering, black women's rights are important to me. Historically, black people have had to fight for their rights in many circumstances. They have struggled for equality even after slavery was abolished, even after *Brown v. Board of Education*, even after the Civil Rights Movement, and the struggle for fair treatment continues today.

When it comes to equal rights for women, the battles have ebbed and flowed throughout history, and in the early 20th century, American feminists won the right to vote. Later, after World War II, more conflict erupted over female sexuality, reproductive rights, family structure, and gender roles and responsibilities. Plus, women had gained a foothold in the workplace while men served in the armed forces, and when the men came home, women were expected to quit and return to their homemaker roles, which created friction for many. More recently, gender discrimination, comparable pay for women, and sexual harassment in the workplace are hot topics of discussion and even lawsuits.[1]

Unfortunately, when women are employed in engineering positions, they endure discrimination that white male engineers do not have to face.[2] It saddens me to say that I have experienced this discrimination that so many other women have borne. You'd think all people would be treated fairly and respectfully today, after so many battles and with so much information available, but that's not the case. I'm not saying we haven't made great strides or that we have no equality at all. Many organizations genuinely embrace diversity and are committed to fair treatment for all. But even so, discrimination, hatred, and racism unfortunately remain common.

This book can't erase enormous social problems like inequality and inequity, but my hope is that it provides women and people of color *meaningful strategies for survival* in the workplace. With so many of us experiencing situations similar to my own, I know that the skills to navigate through them successfully are much needed. Some of us give up, remain silent, and take the treatment. Others quit jobs with high potential and settle into some other, more traditional role. But for those of you reading this book, you don't have to give up. You don't have to sit in silence. You can stand up for yourself, strong and proud, and let them know you're qualified and will be treated respectfully. The tactics in this book will help you navigate your way through many tough situations.

This book is for all the black girls, women, and underrepresented minorities who may have to deal with inequality at work or in any other place, for that matter. If you have been ignored, disrespected, or devalued in the workplace because of your appearance or your cultural background, this book is for you. Finally, if you're a student about to graduate and enter the workforce, you may also find this book helpful.

Acknowledgments

Thank you, God, for your unconditional love. I am so grateful for your guidance and protection. Thank you for being with me everywhere I go.

To my family and friends, thank you for putting up with me and my venting sessions. I appreciate every listening ear, every shoulder I leaned on, and every encouraging and supportive gesture. Thanks for having my back!

Finally, I would like to thank everyone who may have ever disrespected or devalued me. Thank you to the individuals who have counted me out. Thank you to those who did not believe in me. You have taught me valuable lessons that have worked out for my good. You could not break me or tear me down.

Conqueror

Introduction

Being black in America is tough. Well, imagine being black, female, and a millennial in corporate America. Try being a young woman of color in a professional working environment led primarily by middle-aged and older white men. Now, *that* is tough.

After graduating from North Carolina A&T State University with a B.S. in electrical engineering, I went straight into the workforce. I was ready, or so I thought. I mean, I had earned a degree in my chosen field, and I had internalized my parents' teachings: always be on time, be ready to work, never give excuses, meet deadlines, dress appropriately, behave in a professional manner, and be polite to my colleagues. I even had two summer internships at major companies. However, the technical preparation and experience plus the necessary soft skills did not prepare me for the adversity I'd face as an African American woman in the workplace.

I wasn't naive. I knew how African Americans are typically viewed and treated in various situations including the workplace. And I'd always been told that black people must work twice as hard and be twice as smart as our white counterparts if we want to be seen as equal. My challenge was that I'd never exerted extra effort to be considered equal. I had heard of workplace discrimination against minorities, of course, and I was all too familiar with how African Americans have been treated historically. However, I had never, until after college, experienced certain challenges myself in a professional working environment.

But now, in my seven years of professional experience, I've experienced disrespect, discrimination, harassment, and inequality. Engineering, after all, remains dominated by Caucasian men although women and people of color are making advances in the field. Fortunately, countless initiatives have been established to diversify the field of engineering and STEM in general. Some programs start at the K-12 level whereas others focus on the undergraduate and graduate level. Additional programs aim to teach black girls about engineering and how to get there, but they don't teach us how to deal with the challenges underrepresented minorities will face. Nowhere had I been taught how to respond to a leader in a professional environment who tells me, "You're being a bitch" (more on this later).

To press past these challenges, I had to learn from experience and from others who have encountered the same issues. I also had to rely on my faith—it's only because of God's guidance and grace that I've been able to endure these trials. And I'm writing this book because I feel that God placed it on my heart to provide a resource for girls and women like me who have or will encounter poor treatment and difficult situations in the workplace based on who they are or how they look. I've seen so many of my friends go through similar situations. Many of them would make posts on social media detailing their frustrations with being judged or mistreated because of their race or even age.

When I was a little girl, I had friends who were white. In fact, during my primary years, a lot of my friends were white. My best friend was a white girl named Amber. Amber Walton. She lived about five miles from me and we would often visit each other's home. We would travel with each other's families and play together. One day we set up our own lemonade stand and sold lemonade on the side of the road. I even went to church with her family on Tuesday nights. At that time, I was never exposed to racism; we saw each other as equals. We were just two girls who enjoyed playing together. She was not better than me and I was not better than her. I had several other friends who were white, and I didn't think anything of it. Little did I know that later on in life, I would be treated differently than her because she was white and I was black.

It was not until middle school that I started to notice a distinction in race. One of my black classmates asked me why I talked like I was white. This really baffled me because I didn't understand what "talking like I was white" meant. Apparently speaking in the standard English language was "talking like I was white." Since I was not speaking in Ebonics 24/7, I was "acting or talking white." It wasn't long after that when I started to see white and black clearly as separate entities.

The separation of the white kids from the black kids also became more apparent. In high school, my white classmates sat with each other at the lunch tables, and my black classmates formed their own groups. True, some integration existed, but the self-imposed, seemingly natural segregation was apparent. Regardless, I remained friends with both my white and black classmates.

Fast forward—we've had an African American president, we're over 100 years removed from slavery and about 60 years removed from the era of Jim Crow Laws. In the May 17, 1954 decision in *Brown v. Board of Education*, the U.S. Supreme Court ruled that segregation of America's public schools was unconstitutional, and schools have since been integrated. We've been through the Civil Rights Movement of the 1960s, and we've seen the Montgomery bus boycotts, the March on Washington, the Birmingham demonstrations, and countless other outcries for fair treatment and equality since then. Many still alive today remember the assassination of Dr. Martin Luther King Jr., and by now, we should be in a place where people are not judged by the color of their skin. However, in our country today, racial tensions are higher than ever.

What does that mean for us women and people of color in STEM and many other workplaces? Let's take a look.

Into the Workplace

The way our society is structured and how we behave translates directly into the treatment individuals experience in the workplace. The same racist people who do not believe African Americans are as smart as other races or that women cannot lead are the CEOs, the recruiting managers, and the supervisors of organizations. They're team leaders and even your colleagues, and they're doctors, public defenders, teachers, and restaurant employees. Despite official stances of the U.S. Equal Employment Opportunity Commission (EEOC), despite equal opportunity diversity goals, and despite the inclusive culture statement that companies and organizations highlight on their websites, there are still individuals within these groups with negative views of people who are different from them. They take discriminatory actions against minorities or treat them as inferior to the "majority."

Let's look at the structure of our country and the leadership model in place. The current president of the United States (a.k.a. "45"), is basically the boss, the political leader and the chief executive officer of the country. He is the commander in chief, and the number one man in charge.

The president exhibits actions and speech that reveal his view that he and people like him are superior to others. He has referred to a Hispanic Miss Universe as "Miss Housekeeping" and stated that black immigrants from Haiti "all have AIDS" and that once Nigerians see the United States, they would never "go back to their huts" in Africa.[3]

45 appears interested only in himself and clearly holds racist views despite his denials or apparent friendship with black celebrities such as Kanye West or Omarosa Manigault Newman— and we see how this has turned out for them. And from time to time, he attempts to appear supportive of young black people as in his statements at the 2018 Young Black Leadership Summit.[4] Whether he's pandering to his primarily white constituency then covering up or not doesn't matter—whether his private beliefs may or may not be racist, his actions fulfill any definition of racism.

He attacks people of color with words. He has called Omarosa "a dog." Referred to Don Lemon as the "dumbest man on television" and stated that Don Lemon made Lebron James "look smart, which isn't easy to do."[5] These comments are outright racist, considering America's history of racial inferiority.

The Oxford Dictionary defines racist as "a person who shows or feels discrimination or prejudice against people of other races, or who believes that a particular race is superior to another." So, with the "boss" of the country meeting that definition, it is safe to say we have a racist in charge, a racist leading the country and promoting his values.

Now consider this. If you know a certain CEO holds racist beliefs and treats others according to that view, what would that suggest about the company's key leaders and management? The company might include diversity and inclusion statements on every page of their website, and the human resources department might feature diversity posters on every wall. Plus, your employee paperwork or contract will include all appropriate legal statements concerning the company's obligations and your rights as a member of a minority group. But what will reality look like? How will you feel when you're passed over for a promotion? When you learn your pay is much lower than that of a white, male employee in the same role? When the advancement opportunity door slams in your face? When you have no role model, few allies, and the conference room goes silent when you walk in?

The United States is composed of people who immigrated from all parts of the world and we can't forget the descendants of Native Americans who were here first. The citizens of the United States come in all possible sizes, shapes, and colors. Some people look like "45." There are also people who do not look like 45, people with a different skin color or hair texture and those who speak a different language. And all those people embrace many different views and opinions. Despite these differences, any president is, nevertheless, the leader of these unique and diverse individuals.

Now let's remember that the United States was established with a set of principles set forth in The Declaration of Independence, and it's governed by a set of laws and amendments to those laws in both the Constitution of the United States and the Bill of Rights. All three of those documents were created long before the current presidential administration. They were also created prior to the abolishment of slavery and long before blacks and women were allowed to vote, so I argue that they were written with one group of people and one gender in mind, and an amendment to that issue should be made; however, that's a debate for a different book.

Let's examine these two documents briefly and see how they apply to the challenges we face in the present. The Declaration of Independence formally declared the United States' separation from Great Britain. It was signed in 1776 and consists of a set of ideals and principles that our country is founded upon. The Declaration of Independence states:

> *"We hold these truths to be self-evident, that **all men are created equal**, that they are endowed by their Creator with certain unalienable Rights, that among these are Life, Liberty and the pursuit of Happiness. — That to secure these rights, Governments are instituted among Men, deriving their just powers from the consent of the governed, — That whenever any Form of Government becomes destructive of these ends, it is the Right of the People to alter or to abolish it, and to institute new Government, laying its foundation on such principles and organizing its powers in such form, as to them shall seem most likely to effect their Safety and Happiness."[6]*

The Constitution, which holds legal authority, is the sovereign law of the United States. The 14th Amendment to the Constitution states:

> *"All persons born or naturalized in the United States, and subject to the jurisdiction thereof, are citizens of the United States and of the State*

*wherein they reside. **No State shall make or enforce any law which shall abridge the privileges or immunities of citizens of the United States; nor shall any State deprive any person of life, liberty, or property, without due process of law; nor deny to any person within its jurisdiction the equal protection of the laws.**"[7]*

The excerpts above apply to the United States of America and are intended as a guide to governing it; however, the leader of the United States of America clearly does not hold the same values and principles as indicated in the documents. Even though "all men are created equal," our current president supports white supremacist groups, whom he referred to as "very fine people" in light of the rallies and protests that resulted in injuries and a fatality in Charlottesville, VA in 2017.

Despite the law that states no person shall be deprived "of life, liberty, or property, without due process of law," this man urged police officers to violate the rights of suspects in their custody. In a speech to police officials, he said, "Like when you guys put somebody in the car and you're protecting their head...You can take the hand away, OK?"[8] Black people are already treated with hostility when approached by the police in comparison to white people, so comments like these celebrate corruption by the people who are supposed to uphold the law.

That, my people, is how the United States currently operates. I'm sure you can think of other discriminatory actions or situations, now and in the past. And the stage is set by our leaders. Historically, the United States has systemically implemented racism through policies and laws at the federal level; for example, blacks did not have the full right to vote until 1965. Many would argue today that it is still being done with policies that are inflicting voter suppression.

But just these few examples—there are so many more—depict the inequality, prejudice, and racism in this country that can also be found in the American workplace. If leaders and their bigotry are tolerated, it will be found elsewhere. Yes, bigotry and the actions associated with it already existed, but many strides have been made toward improvement. And now, as it trickles down into our local government organizations, political and educational systems, and even in our communities, it's as if silent permission has been granted from up above. Or as if conditions are suddenly right for a latent disease called prejudice to fester and become rampant. And just as children follow their parents' examples, citizens are also influenced, for better or for worse, by their political leaders.

Now historically, when speaking of discrimination, we might immediately think of race and racial differences. But discrimination isn't limited to race. It may be based on gender, age, tenure, socioeconomic group, or educational background. I recently attended a wedding, and the man seated beside me at the reception was a high school teacher. After everyone introduced themselves, I asked him what he taught, and soon we were engulfed in a conversation about STEM education and obstacles we've both faced as young professionals in the workplace. To my surprise, he spoke of his challenges as a young male teacher. It had never occurred to me that male teachers may experience issues within education; however, it happens because most K-12 educators are female. His colleagues, who were mostly women of the same race with many years of experience, treated him as an outsider. They did not approve of some of the approaches he took to reach the students and occasionally left him out.

When bigotry is found in the workplace, discrimination and even harassment follows. Discrimination is illegal today—although that wasn't always the case, but that doesn't mean it doesn't exist. If there are racist employees and supervisors, there is likely some type of discrimination or harassment accompanying it. Individuals will be judged, second-guessed, and mistreated, and sometimes it's hardly noticeable until it becomes a pattern. In a 2017 study, researchers found that when it comes to hiring, there has been no change in the levels of racial discrimination, specifically towards black people, since 1989.[9] And if discrimination in hiring exists, then I am sure that promotions and company benefit decisions will be affected, too. Respect will be selective, and hostile environments will be created just as there are hostile environments within our government.

But what can we do about it? How can we take a stance? Can we change anything? As an electrical engineer, I have worked in environments where I've been surrounded by people who didn't look like me. I was and still am to this day, in certain circumstances, treated differently. As a team of researchers note, "Studies of STEM professionals have found that women encounter numerous challenges in hiring and performance reviews due to implicit bias. These challenges are often multiplied for women of color, who are typically held to stricter standards of competence than whites and are less likely to be recognized for their skills."[10]

They also found that challenges expressed by female engineers of color include:

- *Lack of role models for minority female engineers*
- *Disillusionment regarding the level of impact they would have as engineers*
- *Gender and racial biases and stereotypes experienced in the workplace*
- *Dissatisfaction with salary and benefits*
- *Unfair performance evaluations and lack of honest feedback*
- *Difficulty obtaining professional development through employers*[11]

But this discrimination and mistreatment does not stop in the workplace. It happens in schools, universities, and healthcare facilities. Students are overlooked for awards and recognition because of their race, national origin, religion, and many other factors. African Americans are not always given the same standard of medical care in doctor's offices and in hospitals. On any given day, the media reports how people of color have been denied jobs and promotions or how they've been harassed. Countless documentaries, even Ted Talks, describe this phenomenon and propose solutions[12], and disparities among African Americans and how they are treated are well documented.

You might be wondering, *well what makes you qualified to talk about mistreatment and racism in the workplace?* And here is my answer for you: I have experienced it. And I've found ways to conquer it.

My Story

Let me tell you a little more about myself. I'm a small-town girl. I was born and raised in Ahoskie, a tiny community in northeastern North Carolina. Since I was young, I've always been outgoing and active, participating in various sports, clubs, and volunteer activities. My mother always made sure we were busy to keep us out of trouble, and I sincerely thank her for that. It allowed me to gain valuable experiences that afforded me lessons that I often refer to today.

As I mentioned earlier, I attended North Carolina A&T and received a B.S. in electrical engineering. *Aggie Pride!* While at A&T, I was very involved and participated in as much as I could. I was a dancer and baton twirler—*Golden Delight*—in the university's marching band. I was an academic success coach to freshman students and a member of the National Society of Black Engineers (NSBE). I also was initiated into Alpha Kappa Alpha Sorority, Incorporated (AKA).

After graduating in May of 2011, I launched my career and landed my first job in an organization that develops aircraft systems. I began in a developmental program that consisted of rotational assignments throughout the organization and learning activities through mentoring, training, and events.

The organization was composed primarily of white men

with most of them retired military and middle-aged: anywhere from 45 to 65 years old. A few of my peers in the developmental program looked like me; however, I didn't work with them directly, and our time together was limited to specific events. After graduating from the developmental program, I landed a position as the lead systems engineer on an interdisciplinary team.

My team consisted of individuals who also held other leadership positions, including a program manager, a logistician lead, a budget manager, and a lead contracting officer. All these positions were filled by white men over the age of 50. All of them had served or were currently serving in the military. Imagine it: a young woman fresh out of college, working on a team of military men, men who acted like they were still in the military giving orders to their subordinates.

On top of that, I was usually the only African American millennial female at the meetings I attended. I didn't let that stop me from doing my job, however. I performed well, managing the engineering activities of the program in addition to the work of ten other engineers who reported to me.

My time with that organization lasted four and a half years. I then moved to an organization that focused on medical device development and safety. Starting that job was like a breath of fresh air. Right off the bat, I noticed it was different from my previous position because it was more diverse. I was surrounded by people from all walks of life and varying in race, gender, religion, age, and background. I was thrilled with my new environment.

I was also excited to have an immediate supervisor who was a woman of color. She was deeply knowledgeable and a great leader, and she truly cared about the well-being of her employees. From the beginning, she looked to me for my expertise in electrical engineering. In this new position, I became the subject matter expert, my colleagues came to me for my knowledge, and I was given responsibility without the micromanagement I had previously experienced. My colleagues even referred other employees to me with issues they believed I could help them solve. What a difference.

But even though I excelled at both companies, neither position came without challenge. I experienced some glorious highs, but I also went through a few difficult, stressful lows. Some of you may be able to relate to my experiences while others may not. Either way, I hope you reflect on your own unique situations as I recount some of my more detailed memories.

My Experiences in the Workplace

The Micromanager

"Joe," my colleague and non-engineer, was a micromanager to the nth degree, and his standard operating procedure was to nit-pick, criticize, and find fault with me. It was as if he thought I wasn't doing my job. He would clock the time I arrived to work each day and, if I arrived five minutes later than my typical arrival time, he would make some sort of comment like, "You're running late this morning, huh, Miss Paige?" We sat in close proximity, so he always knew when I arrived and when I left my office, Monday to Friday, all day, every day. It was easy for him to visit to see what I was working on, and he did just that quite often. He would check on my progress with engineering tasks (which he knew little about), and he'd even reach out to the engineers on my team, which was a clear overstep of boundaries.

I'm not sure what triggered his insecurities, but I'm drawn to believe it's because I'm not a typical engineer. I'm petite in frame and I was young in age, and I probably appeared to him as a "little black girl." I mean, I *was* a twenty-something-year-old, a few years removed from college. Maybe he just couldn't believe such a "little girl," and black on top of it, had so much responsibility.

One day, Joe decided to raise his voice at me in the office. He was upset when he found out I made my travel arrangements for a work trip without consulting with him. He wasn't even my supervisor, and I couldn't believe this. *Travel?! He's raising his voice at me in the office about travel?*

I think Joe fully expected me to stand there and take that verbal "beat down." I sternly replied and informed him that 1) he does not have to raise his voice at me and speak to me in a demeaning manner since we are professionals in a work environment; 2) I am a competent adult who can work independently and book travel-related work independently; 3) if he had an issue with me booking travel or if he wished he'd been informed so he could travel with me, then he should have simply approached me in a professional manner and let it be known since I wasn't privy to his expectations.

I think he was shocked to hear me speak so firmly as were others nearby who saw and overheard the entire exchange. A couple of my colleagues approached me afterward and praised me on how I stood up for myself and handled the situation. I definitely was not looking for praise, but I was looking for respect. I got my respect that day.

After our run-in, I walked back to my office, and I think Joe must have marinated on what I had said. He visited my desk, apologized, and explained why he wanted to be aware of my travel plans. We had a conversation about his behavior on that day and prior days. I brought up his micromanaging and discussed roles and responsibilities. After the encounter, Joe's attitude toward me changed, and we were able to express our concerns; the tense feelings that I had towards him went away and we actually became closer in a way. He would look out for me and stand up for me when it came to other people who treated me differently or who were not confident in my work. We met with various individuals within the organization to discuss our work and, since he was with the organization longer, he was more familiar with the individuals we worked with. I was grateful for that support and for someone who could vouch for me. I learned to keep him updated more on the status of my projects with boundaries set. We were, after all, on the same team, and some moments almost reminded me of a father-daughter relationship. That might sound weird, but he did take me under his wing, so to speak. I think deep down he wanted the best for me and the team; however, his initial way of making that known was difficult. It upset me, and it created a lot of stress—it was certainly not ideal.

Lack of Trust

I have to give you a little background information first before getting into another scenario that took place. The next level of leadership above my program manager was the department head and assistant department head. After my program manager reviews completed work, the departmental level head does a final review before publication which is typically cursory, not comprehensive or in-depth.

But here's what happened on one occasion.

The assistant department head, "Sarah," was reviewing one of my work products, which was detailed extensively in a report. Sarah forwarded it via email to an electrical engineer from another team, which was not standard procedure.

The particular engineer called upon to review my work, "Lin," has been at the organization for many years. Sarah asked for his opinion and whether a certain concern I had raised was appropriate since she didn't think it was. Keep in mind that Sarah is not an electrical engineer and does not have expertise in the area.

Sarah hadn't approached me about my work nor did she include me on the email to Lin or even inform me that she was reaching out to him. Lin replied to Sarah, however, and he copied me on the email. In his reply, Lin indicated that he reviewed my report and supports my proposal recommendations. His email actually praised my work.

Y'all, excuse the Southern in me, but when I first saw that chain of emails, I was like, "Oh. My. Goodness. Did she really just try to go behind my back?" But when I saw Lin's response, I was like "Oh yeaaaah!" Unbeknownst to Sarah, Lin and I had worked together previously, and he had actually mentored me early on. Since Lin copied me on the email, I was able to view the email chain and could see all of her original messages exposing her judgments about me.

In essence, Sarah didn't think I was capable of doing my job and thought my work was incorrect. Was it because she simply assumed I wasn't knowledgeable? Well, that doesn't seem likely since I have a degree in electrical engineering, took training courses when I first started the position, had a mentor, and I had been doing the work for a while at that point. I was not brand new, and I had been producing quality work all along, which she knew. With that in mind, instead of immediately reaching out to someone else, she should have talked with me, first, if she were truly concerned. This was one of many incidents in which I was second-guessed, but this particular display of bias was minute compared to another situation.

One of Those Situations You'll Never Forget

One day, the department head—a man—said to me, "You're being a bitch." Now I'm sure you're wondering how we got to that moment and, for the life of me, I'm still trying to figure that one out, too.

Some of you may say, *Oh that's nothing. I've experienced worse.* And that may be true. There are individuals who are physically and sexually harassed in the workplace, and I have deep sympathy for them. If that's happening to you, I urge you to remove yourself from that situation and get help.

But as for my situation, I had never before had anyone

call me out of my name like that in the workplace. For me, it was unreal, especially because I was in a professional environment at work where people should be able to work without any major concerns. It's still unbelievable to me to this day that he positioned his lips to call me that. So here is the story from the beginning to give you the necessary context.

At this particular job, everyone has an office. The type of office an employee is assigned is governed by guidelines developed by the Facilities Office of the organization. To that end, a list is maintained in which all employees are ranked based on their tenure, salary, number of days working in their current office, and a few other factors. If you're at the top of the list and a better office becomes available, then you're eligible to move into that office if you choose. If multiple offices are available, you get to choose which one you would like based on your ranking.

Well, my turn finally came. I was at the top of the list, and four new single offices were available. So, I had priority over the individuals who were ranked under me, and I was finally able to select the office of my choice first. I was thrilled.

"Joseph," the department head, showed me all four offices to choose from. I selected one, and I also followed up via email with the office room number to avoid any misunderstanding, as there had been "misunderstandings" with Joseph before, not only with me but with my African American colleagues. We had all experienced mix-ups regarding him actually doing what he says he will do—or not.

On the day I picked up my key to move into my new office, the key didn't work. I checked with the secretary who had issued the key, and she said I was trying to get into the wrong office. Apparently, I was assigned an office that wasn't even shown or offered to me. When I told the secretary what offices I was shown and what office I was supposed to occupy, she told me that the offices I'd seen weren't in my department. *Hmm, this isn't making sense*, I thought, and I investigated.

I talked to my colleagues who were also up for moving into the other three offices, and I found out that Joseph had shown them a different set of offices than he showed me. So, I was given an office I could neither accept nor decline. I was put in a tough position because I didn't want to create a rift with my coworkers; I didn't want to kick them out of an office that they were promised had already started moving in to.

So I let it go. I would be moving into a single office, I reasoned, and that was fine with me. It was better than sharing as I had been, at least, even though it wasn't what I had chosen. And I was not going to fret over an office, which is miniscule compared to other things in life.

What really bothered me, though, was how Joseph had handled the situation. He had not followed the Facilities Office guidelines, and what he had done was really unethical. He had actually told me not to tell anyone that he was showing me the offices because there were issues which he did not elaborate further on. When I think about that retrospectively, I know that him telling me to "keep a secret" about him showing me the offices was very suspicious, and I probably should have alerted the Facilities Office. He had a history, after all, of going about things inappropriately, specifically when it came to allowing individuals to be moved into new offices. My colleagues have had issues in the past where he allowed his favorites to be moved instead of going by the guidelines.

Treat everyone fairly; that's my motto. As a leader, you

have to be honest and have integrity if you want to maintain team morale and encourage productivity. So I planned to speak to Joseph about the situation privately and express my concerns. I intended to talk to him about the Facilities Office guidelines and to discuss transparency in situations that impact me. I had not planned to argue or fuss since that's not my style. In fact, I don't like conflict at all, but I will stand up for myself when needed. I will not be a pushover or a doormat or let people take advantage of me.

So, a day or so later, I waited in the hallway for a meeting with my supervisor who was finishing up with someone else. Joseph walked by me, stepped into his office to grab something, and he walked back out. While he moved in and out of his office, he started a dialogue that went something like this:

Joseph, the department head: *Hey, how's the new office? Getting all those boxes unpacked?* (He continued to walk in and out of his office as he is talking.)
Me: *Yes, but I wanted to have a conversation with you about that.*
Joseph: *What's wrong? Isn't it good enough? Do you want to move into a different one? Pick which one you want and move into any of the other ones.* (He continues to walk away while talking.)
Me: *But they've all been selected and assigned to people now.*
Joseph: *Well, that's okay, you can move, and we'll tell them. I'll tell the people upstairs that you're being a bitch.*
Me: *Well, that's not the issue. I think you went about it the wrong way...* (I stopped talking as I processed what he just said to me.)

<u>Joseph</u>: *I'll come down and talk to you later.* (He departs up the stairs.)

As a side note, I think "the people upstairs" he referred to is the Facilities Office. He's supposed to inform a Facilities representative, who sits upstairs, of office moves. But forget who the people upstairs are, why would he refer to me in that derogatory way?

My Initial Reaction

I was in shock after that brief and swift exchange. I literally was left standing there thinking, "Did he really just say what I thought he said?" I thought my ears were deceiving me. Did he just say the b-word? Did he just call me the b-word? *In my Southern accent*: Y'alllll, I am a kind, soft-spoken individual. I do not go around disrespecting people. In the workplace, I am polite to everyone, friendly, and I do my work in a timely manner with accuracy. I am an exceptional employee, and that is not just my own self-assessment. My performance reviews have all indicated that I'm an exceptional employee. I have also received awards and recognitions for my work and ability to work on diverse teams. I have receipts, so to speak, and to be called something I am not was unexpected and appalling.

My supervisor was still meeting with someone behind her closed door, and I couldn't stand there any longer after what just transpired. I went down the hall to a trusted colleague and told her what happened. She was astounded. Puzzled. Shocked. She's much older than me, and she got upset and emotional, which in turn made me emotional. We talked for a few minutes, but I tried to pull it together, and I went to my one-on-one meeting with my supervisor.

I could not hold back my emotions, and I was visibly upset. It's exceedingly difficult for me to hide my emotions sometimes, and there was no need to try. Trying to compose myself and hold back tears, I told my supervisor everything leading up to the conversation that had just ensued with Joseph. She apologized for what I experienced. She asked if there was anything she could do. She was incredibly supportive and upset by what happened and wanted to do whatever she could to help me.

Some of you are probably wondering why I started crying. I don't know why I cried, and I asked myself the same thing. Maybe because my colleague did. Maybe it was the stress of everything else going on in my life. Generally, I'm tough when it comes to situations like that, and it's not like I've been sheltered all my life and never encountered conflict. There were girls who didn't like me in high school and consistently made it known by hurling mean words and threats in the hallways. I've had people tell me I'd never be able to do this or that. I have had doors closed on me, I've been cursed out, and I've probably been called every negative name in the book, but I've always remained resilient. So why did this upset me to the point of crying?

I found myself wondering why I got so emotional. I thought, well, I have probably never experienced a boss disrespect me to my face like that. Was it because he was white? Did I let my guard down when it should have been up? Or was it because I got a small taste of how my ancestors or even present-day brothers and sisters are treated because of racism? Since this whole incident stems from what I believe is some type of

32

discrimination, part of me thinks this affected me at a different level than anything else I had experienced in the past. Mistreatment and inequality because of who you are or what you look like, all factors you can't control, hits you from a different level. So, the best explanation I can give you is that I was hurt. Hurt that I was treated that way. Hurt and even mad that people are still being treated that way, and even worse.

One thing I do know for sure is that no matter what name I am called by others, it doesn't matter because I know who I am and whose I am. I am God's child (Galatians 3:26). I am more than a conqueror through Him who loves me (Romans 8:37). I am the light of the world (Matthew 5:14). And you're special, too, no matter what names someone might call you, how you're treated, what you believe, or what faith you follow. You and I are worthy of respect.

What I Did Next

I spoke to a representative from the Facilities Office that same day to tell her what happened. She suggested that I talk to Joseph face-to-face and tell him that his behavior was unacceptable. This made sense, and I decided I would face him. I asked my supervisor to sit in with me on a conversation with Joseph and she agreed. I felt her attendance was necessary not only for support but because I did not trust Joseph, and I needed a witness in case anything else inappropriate occurred. The conversation did not happen that same day but the next because of availability. I actually was glad it happened the next day because it gave me time to calm down and reflect on what had happened.

As I mentioned earlier, I don't like conflict, but that meeting had to be held. His actions had to be addressed. Even though it was difficult for me, I knew I had to face him. He had probably done this before and gotten away with it, but I had to stand up for myself and let him know that I was not going to be treated or disrespected in that way.

I started the meeting by informing him that when he used a derogatory word to address me the prior day in the hallway, I was offended. I told him that was unacceptable and inappropriate in the workplace, especially coming from a leader. He apologized immediately and said that it would never happen again.

Sounds good, doesn't it? Well, you won't believe what happened next. This man turned red; I mean his face turned bright red, and he broke down and cried. Now that really threw me for a loop. I'd been worried that *I* would break down and cry, and I thought, *Why is this man crying? Is he for real? Is this to gain some sort of sympathy from me?* I didn't have any sympathy at that point. Knowing me and how my facial expressions typically show how I'm feeling at the moment, I was probably looking at him like he was crazy.

He continued to tell me about personal issues he was having and explained it was a bad day, and that he shouldn't have even come to work. He apologized again and asked to keep "this" between us. Well, folks, I'm obviously telling you what happened, so I definitely didn't keep it "between us."

And you know what? He was scared. I say this because he came back and apologized to me two more times after that, crying again during one of those follow-up apologies. I figured he had really thought about his actions and how they could impact

34

his job. But did he care how his actions impacted me?

Let's talk about the conversation that took place a little more. He apologized, which was acceptable. But giving excuses and blaming personal issues as the reason for calling me out of my name is not! As a leader, you have to know how to handle your emotions and work under pressure. Leaders are looked up to and held to a higher standard, and he had no excuse for the type of behavior he displayed. We all have issues and hard times; I understand that. I go to work stressed out sometimes, too, as we all do. But I don't take my problems and frustrations out on others in the workplace, and I definitely don't call people the b-word or any other nasty names.

I think he assumed I would accept what he'd offered, and everything would go back to the status quo. No sir. Not me. I was already talking to the Facilities Office about submitting a formal grievance and about options for filing an EEO or harassment complaint. This behavior was unacceptable. If the situation was the other way around, I'm sure he wouldn't want an African American man calling his daughter the b-word. If the shoes were on the opposite feet, I'm positive he would have called the dogs on him very quickly.

After my conversation with Joseph, I spoke to the Facilities Office vice president and learned about all my options as far as reporting this behavior. His behavior is considered harassment, plus he has a history of being biased towards other employees. For those reasons, I wanted to make sure that someone in leadership above him knew what was going on.

This was a tough decision for me, and I sought out advice from others. Responses varied. Some individuals thought I should file an EEO complaint and sue the organization. They suggested I build up a case, go to multiple counseling sessions and say that it has caused me stress and anxiety in the workplace. To me that sounded sort of outrageous. Cases like that take time and a lot of effort. I mean, I was fine. I've been called bad names before and I have bounced back. It just seemed like a long, drawn-out route to take, and I was interested in moving on swiftly. Some even suggested that I just do nothing, but I wasn't having that, either. Something had to be done. I consulted with the program management director with the intention of getting advice on what to do. She told me that, due to her particular position in the organization, she was required to tell his boss what happened since I told her. She explained that Joseph's boss would take action, but it was still my choice to pursue other courses of action.

All of this advice was very confusing. At the end of the day, I had to make a decision that was the best decision for me. I prayed about it, and I came to the conclusion that we all have bad days, we all make mistakes and act out of character. I also believe that we all deserve second chances. God gives us grace and mercy and for me, I had to forgive my department lead and move on. I chose forgiveness.

Since the program management office was going to inform Joseph's supervisor, I felt that was enough, and I decided not to take any additional action. I didn't want to go through the lengthy process of filing a grievance or formal suit. But one thing I did tell myself was that if something like this ever happened again, I would definitely submit a formal grievance or complaint.

After Joseph's boss was made aware of what happened, he wanted to meet with me personally. He apologized and also indicated he would take action. I was not privy to the type of punishment or reprimand that Joseph received, but I noticed he wasn't around for a while. And when he returned, his behavior definitely changed towards me. It seemed like he was nicer, and whatever happened surely made him fix his behavior.

Reflecting on the situation, I still am confident in my decision. But there are times when I have wondered if I made the right decision. Should I have filed a formal complaint? Was I too forgiving? Forgiveness is hard, let me say that, but you do it for yourself and not for others. We also forgive others as God in Christ has forgiven us (Ephesians 4:32). We have all sinned against God and others and have been given forgiveness, so we must offer it up to others.

In the process of writing this book, and with the incident happening a long time ago, I still think about the outcome. I was in a recent training course, and we were discussing conflict management. We had to recall a personal conflict we had encountered in the workplace and do an activity. Of course, this is the conflict that came to mind. The activity consisted of writing down what the conflict was about, strategies used to address the conflict, the outcome, and my level of satisfaction with the outcome. The main strategy I used was confrontation. The outcome was an apology from Joseph, but I did not know what specific consequences he faced from his management. I found myself wanting to know what happened to him because, if it wasn't good enough, maybe I needed to go and report him to someone else so they could punish him some more. This was terrible thinking!

But something I had heard from the renowned Pastor TD Jakes came to mind. He said, "If you seek revenge, God can't do his justice." That really resonated with me. Let me say it again, "If you seek revenge, God can't do his justice." I still wondered what happened to Joseph, but I realized it was not for me to know. I couldn't be concerned with that. It was not right for me to want something bad to happen to him because he did me wrong. I couldn't seek revenge on this man. I couldn't aim to hurt him. I must leave that up to God and those who have authority over him. I had addressed the situation directly, he apologized, and his manager was also informed and took action. That was enough.

This experience and others have helped to shape me and make me more resilient. So many lessons have come from this and other situations, and even though I may be counted out, judged not good enough, or treated differently than my counterparts, I will keep pushing. I will succeed, and I won't be stopped because of the insecurities of others. I can say that this situation was one of those that stand out for me. There have been other experiences here and there, but this was one of those where I was blatantly disrespected. But I didn't let it stop me. I didn't quit my job. Yeah, I cried a little bit, but I stood up for myself. It was difficult, but I didn't run. I decided to stand up and be a conqueror.

A Conqueror: Part I

Yet in all these things we are more than conquerors
through Him who loved us.
-Romans 8:37

So, what do I mean when I say *be a conqueror*? Well, I mean that I will not let people filled with hatred and insecurities affect me. I will not let people who treat me differently or try to hold me back drive me out or force me away from something I love or am working towards. You can be a conqueror, too.

Now, at the beginning of this book, I spoke about how I was not prepared for what I would encounter in terms of inequality in the workplace. I stated that I was prepared technically but I was not ready for the challenges of being mistreated because of my race, age, or gender. I had attended a Historically Black College and University (HBCU), but there were no classes on "being a minority in the workplace." If there were, I completely missed them. Sure, I gained valuable skills like the technical knowledge needed in my field, a certain degree of resilience, and teamwork experience. My HBCU even instilled in me a keen sense of community and pride.

I had also absorbed the harsh realities that black college students faced years ago because of the color of their skin, and I learned about the A&T Four who stood up for "our" rights. On February 1, 1960, Ezell Blair Jr., Franklin McCain, Joseph McNeil, and David Richmond walked into an all-white lunch counter and sat down. They were critical in the Greensboro sit-ins and the desegregation of Woolworth department stores.

But as I'm writing about it, I'm rethinking my initial assertion. Maybe I did learn a little something that I thought should be taught in a class. Maybe I *was* prepared to deal with racism. Learning about those who had come before me and how they did not accept mistreatment, how they developed opportunities for themselves and broke down walls so that they could have a seat at the table—was this the preparation? Maybe unconsciously I was prepared all along. Maybe my African American history class was that preparation. And the demanding work during my rookie year in the band taught me that I had to work for veteran status and that nothing was going to be handed to me. It showed me that I had to go after what I wanted, but I also had to possess the skills necessary to get it.

As I continue to reflect on my experiences, I realize that I was prepared for the workplace. I was prepared for adversity. I have been preparing all my life. My parents prepared me through sound instruction, discipline, and teaching me that a faithful relationship with Christ would sustain me. They trained me up in the way I should go, and I did not depart from it (Proverbs 22:6). Those mean girls in high school prepared me. They showed me that their words could not stop my success. North Carolina A&T prepared me. Motivation from black women like Oprah, Michelle Obama, and Google executive and North Carolina native Valeisha Butterfield Jones push me to break barriers like they have and continue to do. Knowledge of my ancestors and grandparents plus seeing my family and friends endure tough situations have also played a role in preparing me. I have also learned from my own trials and tribulations. I use failures and times of distress or uncertainty as a learning opportunity.

My journey has not been smooth, but I have learned how to survive and maneuver through places and situations where I have been the minority or treated subpar. My experiences have taught me how to be a conqueror, and I believe the lessons I've learned can help you be a conqueror, too. They can help you overcome people or systems that try to tear you down. But first, you need to understand *why* you want to be a conqueror if that is the path you choose.

Why Conquer?

Before you decide to become a conqueror and refuse to let people or situations stop you from your goals, run you away from that job, or interrupt your progress on whatever it is you may be working towards, you must first know why you want to be a conqueror. If you don't know why, it will be too easy to give up.

You must know your why! Why do you want to fight your way through? Why keep going to a place where you're unappreciated when it's so simple and so much easier to leave? Why not just go do your own thing? Keep reading to find your why.

Because We Do Not Quit

I was raised to always finish what I start. When I wanted to play soccer as a little girl, on the very first day of practice one of the other little girls asked me, "What kind of name is Paige?" She said it sarcastically, with judgment and ridicule in her tone. After that moment, I became extremely withdrawn and did not want to go back to soccer. When I told my mom I wanted to stop, she reminded me that this was something I wanted to do so I wouldn't quit and I would finish the season—*especially since she had already paid, right.*

I didn't tell her the real reason I wanted to quit soccer, but I still was able to learn from that experience. I learned that you do not give up because people may be mean to you, otherwise you'll miss out on a lot of good things. And that summer was one of the best summers I had as a kid. Although things didn't start out well with that other little girl, we eventually became friends, after I set her straight about my name, and I learned a lot about teamwork that year. I also learned to never quit.

When it looks like you're losing the soccer game, that's not the time to quit. It's time to go hard! You play to your fullest potential until the game is over because you never know what the outcome may be. You can come back in the game with the time you have left, as we've seen many times before in basketball, and win. This same lesson applies to life. Never give up when the going gets tough because you're almost there, almost at the receiving line for a reward. That reward could be a lesson learned, a skill gained, or an opportunity presented.

What if Martin Luther King Jr. gave up? What if Harriet

Tubman, Sojourner Truth, and Frederick Douglass gave up? Our ancestors didn't give up. When there were other slaves or family members telling them their actions or plans were crazy and that they'd never make it out, that they'd never succeed, and that they'd always be treated as inferior, they didn't listen. What if they'd taken to heart the worries and fears of others? What if they hadn't continued to fight, to conquer? Where would we be?

If those people who were slaves could go through the torment and the oppression they endured back during the time of slavery, during the Jim Crow Law era, and during the Civil Rights Movement and still come out strong, then I know we can do it. We live in a world where technology and information is right at our fingertips. We have access to the internet, mentors, and training classes, and we can communicate with people to get all the information we need. There is no need to give up on what we want to accomplish. There is no reason for us to quit when someone tells us we can't do it. We have plenty of examples that show that we can do it and that we can do it well. We can exceed the expectations that people may have for us and exceed the bar or level that has been set and establish a new standard. This can happen in all aspects of our lives, not just in the workplace.

What if gymnast Dominique Dawes quit or tennis greats Venus and Serena Williams quit? Black girls who compete in sports that used to be, and sometimes still are, comprised primarily of one ethnic group probably encountered people who discouraged them or treated them differently, but they kept going. I am so grateful my mother instilled in me that "no quitting" philosophy. Although times may get hard and you feel like there is no hope in sight, that is no reason to quit. When you quit, you miss out on things that could benefit you. You miss out on learning opportunities. You miss out on developing skills to persevere through difficult circumstances of all kinds. James 1:2-4 urges you to be joyful when you face challenges because these challenges test your faith and bring forth perseverance. And when you quit, you also miss out on opportunities to impact the lives of others, to be a role model to children and young people, or to pave the way for others.

Sometimes there *is* a time to quit. If you're in a situation that is detrimental to you, whether that be physically, emotionally, or mentally damaging, of course you should quit. Your well-being is a top priority, after all. If you've reached a dead end or a pit where there is clearly no path forward or potential to grow, then that may be a situation you should get out of.

Now if your current place of employment or position simply doesn't fall in line with your passions and desires, then it's okay to quit and move on to where you are called. But before you quit, I urge you to consider what you could gain by remaining in that position temporarily. I believe God puts us in some situations temporarily to learn, grow, and hone skills or lessons that will benefit us in the future. And even if you don't see things exactly my way, you can still choose to learn and grow instead of quitting. Either way, this development process is too important to rush because we may miss out on things that can help us elsewhere. So, I urge you to look for the good in a situation before you abandon it completely. I'll discuss this in the next chapter.

Everywhere You Go Will Have Flaws

No job or situation will ever be perfect in every aspect. I know people who continually bounce from job to job or organization to organization—or relationship to relationship for that matter—because they are always looking for a place (or person) that fits them flawlessly or checks off every box with no issues.

I hate to be the one to break it to you, but utopia does not exist. There will always be "something" everywhere you go. We do not live in a perfect world, there are no perfect people, and no place will be designed to fit a single person's every want and need.

The reality is that we have to make the best of situations we're in. My first job out of college had no diversity whatsoever. There were very few people who looked like me, I was micromanaged by a non-engineer, and I had to fight for my respect. It was a difficult environment, at best, and when I left and went to my second organization, it was like a breath of fresh air. The diversity was obvious, my supervisor was spectacular, and the work I did was awesome. But eventually, the negative aspects came out, as they always do.

On the surface, organizations may seem like they have it all together, but no one does. Where there are people, there are flaws, and the best course of action is to not let these flaws or challenges affect you and your ultimate goals (we will talk about strategies on how to deal with imperfect people and organizations later). You should do your best and work around them or work towards fixing these shortcomings, but running every time something happens isn't the answer. All workplaces fall short of perfection, and you may be running into a place that's worse than the place you left.

You Can Make a Difference and Initiate Change

We are conquerors whether we know it or not, and we all have the potential to do remarkable things. History shows that we, people of color, have broken barriers many times and made significant contributions to our country and world:

- Ida B. Wells was a newspaper editor and journalist. As a founding member of the NAACP, she was a civil rights activist and investigated lynching in the south during the late 19th and early 20th centuries.
- Hattie McDaniel was the first African American to receive an Oscar for best supporting actor in 1939.
- Shirley Chisholm, the first black congresswoman in 1968, campaigned for women's and civil rights.

When you decide you want to be a conqueror, you resolve to stand up for what is right and not let anyone tear you down. You start or continue working in your chosen field, and you're determined to reach your goals and make your way to the top. You *can* make a difference in your organization. Some may ask, *Why not just leave and start your own company?* I'm all for entrepreneurship, but if we *really* want to make change in our society, we've got to be where "they" (white people, the majority of decision makers) are so we can penetrate that invisible wall and be a part of decisions that impact people of color at a systemic level. We can influence how people view us and make organizational changes that benefit everyone.

How else will we change the structure of our country? We need people in places to ensure all people are treated equally.

President Barack Obama was our first African American president, and every day the naysayers criticized him. They disagreed with what he said, with his policies, and with every action he took. People didn't believe in him or support him, and he was often called all sorts of names. It couldn't have been easy for him or his family, but he kept going and kept working for the American people. He put policies in place that impacted black people in a positive way, programs that are now being ripped to shreds by his successor. This is the reason we need people of color and people who truly strive for equality, no matter their race, to be in office and to hold leadership positions in organizations.

If you see issues that may be hindering the growth or production of an organization and/or employees, you can point those things out via employee viewpoint surveys, make suggestions for improvement to management, or even join (or form) an employee relations improvement team within your organization to seek change. A good company is genuinely interested in retaining employees and creating a culture that is inclusive and supportive of employees because those are the best environments for productivity. They should be interested in learning about issues and challenges that hinder workplace efficiency and be open to change.

> "And just as we have the power to shape culture,
> we also have the power to undo the culture that
> does not serve us well. So, let's work together,
> women and men, as a united music industry
> committed to creating more safe work

environments, equal pay, and access for all
women."
—*Janelle Monae*

You Can Obtain Knowledge, Skills, and Abilities that Open the Door to Other Opportunities

I believe there is a lesson in everything. Just like failed relationships can teach you lessons about trust, respect, and teamwork, a strained work environment can provide many lessons. Being in a workplace with people who may treat you differently teaches you how to stand up for yourself and how to treat others. You obtain knowledge about working with distinct types of people and personalities, and you can gain conflict resolution skills that will help you in every facet of life.

Most corporate and government organizations offer training in areas that can benefit you on and off the job, and you should take full advantage of the knowledge, skills, and abilities offered while there. Whether they're formal or informal professional development programs or even just afternoon workshops or online training, jump on the opportunity when offered.

If you have entrepreneurship in your plans, why not take it slow and learn all you can about established organizations instead of jumping ship in a hurry? It can serve as a focused learning opportunity, and you'll gain tons of knowledge on procedures, common practices, and management styles. You can still plan and build your own business slowly in your spare time while making the best of your current position. Use the experience to your advantage until you're truly ready to branch off and do your own thing. Ask questions, get what you need, and move on.

You Can Pave the Way for Others

Remaining with an organization and excelling will put you in a favorable position to pave the way for other minorities and people of color who might not otherwise be judged fairly. I'm sure you're familiar with the saying, "It's not what you know, but who you know." Well, I believe that is true in a sense.

While you must be qualified for a position and possess basic knowledge and a degree of understanding the job, another major component of securing a position today depends on whether the hiring official knows or is acquainted with you and if there are other individuals in the organization who would vouch for you.

One of the main reasons I landed my first job, outside of my qualifications, was because of my AKA sorority sister who was already working at the company. Her manager asked his staff for recommendations for recent graduates, and she forwarded my resume to him. I believe her advocacy helped to influence the hiring decision, and we, too, can serve as advocates for other minorities and people of color by vouching and advocating for them. There is room for all of us to succeed, and we must look out for each other.

I am extremely grateful to my sorority sister because my first job afforded me many opportunities and learning experiences that I appreciate. I moved up the ranks quickly and was eventually assigned to a lead systems engineer role, and I was endorsed by management for the distinguished Black Engineer of the Year award, which I won in 2014 for Community Service. That's not to say my good fortune came easily; it didn't. I worked hard, and I struggled at times, but I didn't quit. I persevered. I conquered.

I've always been a strong proponent of giving back, reaching back, and supporting those who may be from the same place I'm from. "Where I am from" is a broad concept and is different for everyone. It can include my hometown, my cultural background, the university I attended, the society or club in which I was a member, and so on. It can also include early learning experiences, upbringing, family income, and various struggles along the way. And when we help others "where I am from," we may create opportunities and increase our presence in places where few of us work or dare to dream of. This helps to shape organizations and peoples' opinions about us.

Many people view African Americans as criminals or people living in poverty, and the few African Americans they're familiar with are celebrities, athletes, or individuals in the limelight. But oh, if more of us who defy these stereotypes infiltrate the workplace, they would see we're not only people with strong physical or musical abilities, but that we're also intelligent beings who can design and create.

Look at Oprah. She was told she wouldn't succeed; however, she kept going and paved the way for others in the entertainment business. She has inspired women and African Americans who have faced difficult circumstances like sexual abuse or growing up in poverty. She paved the way because she kept going and didn't stop. She showed everyone that people like her can be successful and that success isn't limited to one select group.

I mentioned President Barack Obama earlier. The fact that he broke barriers and became the first African American U.S. president has shown people of color that they, too, can be the president of the United States. He has shown those who view black people only as thugs and less-than-them, that black people are educated and relatable.

We are intelligent people who can do the same things the "majority" does in the workplace and in every other place. We must pave the way and help bring others in so they have opportunities to excel and influence companies. We can show them we are just as smart as them. We can show them we are just as talented as them. We can demonstrate how we get the job done as well as anyone else, often better and even faster. We can change the way they view us and in turn how they treat us, not only because of our on-the-job smarts, but also by our leadership.

Your Personal Why: _____

If you're going to be a conqueror, you need to have your own personal "why," and it might be something I haven't mentioned. Your "why" could be you love what you're doing; it's your passion and you won't let anyone take that from you. Your *why* may be because your livelihood depends on it. Maybe you want to keep pushing through because you have to support others financially or others are relying on you.

Take a moment to reflect and think about *why* you want to conquer the workplace. Fill in the blank above and write a few sentences below or in the space provided at the end of this book on why you want to be a conqueror.

A Conqueror: Part II

So now you know what it means to be a conqueror, from my point of view at least. I hope you've looked deep into yourself and figured out your *why* and made up your mind to push through. Remember, knowing your *why* will help you stay committed to your goal, but I'm not suggesting it's some kind of magic potion. Just because you know your *why* doesn't mean you'll suddenly have an easier time; instead, you'll be challenged. But you'll learn, and you'll grow, and you'll succeed because you'll lean on your *why* to help you stay the course.

For those of you who may be ambivalent about quitting a position or unsure about pressing through a situation, I urge you to contemplate your decision before you make it. You should weigh the pros and cons but also look to God or within your faith and beliefs for guidance. Whatever you decide, whether it be leaving or persisting, don't leave just because the going might get rough, and don't let people run you away. You'll eventually have to tackle the same issues once again. Why not now?

Ultimately, you're the only one who can make this decision for yourself. But gathering food for thought can help you make the best decision possible. Here are a few questions to consider in your decision-making.

1. Is the position or job something you're passionate about and something you love doing?
2. Is the position or job going to help you advance or gain the skills necessary for a new opportunity you're passionate about?
3. Will promotion be possible in a new job?
4. Is the position or job detrimental to your health or the health of others?
5. Is the position or job a dead end (i.e., there is nothing else to learn or gain, there is no benefit to working there other than pay and benefits, there is no opportunity for promotion)?

If you answered yes to the first three questions, consider pushing through. If you answered yes to questions four and five, then pursuing other opportunities may be wise.

If you decide to resolve issues and conquer this job or position, continue reading to learn about strategies and practices that can assist you along the way. If you decide to leave, there's no judgment—only you know what's best for you. That said, keep on reading because, as I said earlier, you'll find flaws everywhere you go. Your next position will have its difficulties just like the last, and what I have to share with you will help.

How to Conquer

Now that you've chosen to carry on in a job where you're not treated fairly or you're treated differently (or if you face these issues in the future), it's time for advice that I believe will help you conquer.

Get Rid of All Excuses

"Excuses are tools of the incompetent that build monuments of nothingness and those who specialize in them seldom amount to anything. Excuses, Excuses, Excuses."
—*Author Unknown*

First things first: you have to get rid of any and all excuses you may have. I had to learn the adage above for the *first* time during my rookie year in my university band. It still rings true in my life today. Excuses are something I try to refrain from using or even saying out loud or thinking about. If you want to be successful in life, you cannot give reason after reason for why you think you can't achieve something. You cannot reach a goal or excel in an organization with a ton of excuses. Just like the adage above says, people who specialize in excuses rarely accomplish anything. You set yourself up for failure when you try to justify why something cannot be achieved.

Some of the top excuses in jobs and careers include: *Those people are too hard to work with. I'm too young. I'm too old. I don't have the credentials. Lots of people already do this, and they don't need me. Women don't work in this field.* Well, excuses are just that: excuses. They aren't solid, logical reasons for any action or inaction; most often they're our innermost fears and worries rising up. Take a look at my responses that dismiss all of them and probably any other excuse you can come up with:

Those people are so hard to work with – Lots of people are difficult. Plus, life isn't fair and there will always be difficult colleagues who try to hinder your progress no matter what color your skin is. But that didn't stop Katherine Johnson who worked with difficult male colleagues during a time where separate but equal educational institutions was legal. Katherine Johnson, played by Taraji P. Henson in the movie *Hidden Figures*, is an African American woman who worked as a NASA mathematician beginning in 1953. She calculated the trajectory for astronaut John Glenn's space flight, and her contributions made the first and subsequent human space flights, orbits, and moon landings possible. President Barack Obama awarded her with the Presidential Medal of Freedom in 2015.

I am too young – At just 11 years old, Mikaila Ulmer created "Me and the Bees Lemonade," which is sold in Starbucks and Whole Foods stores throughout the United States.

I don't have the credentials – Valeisha Butterfield Jones is the Global Head of Women and Black Community Engagement at Google with only a bachelor's degree in political science.

There are already lots of people who do this already and they don't need me – Shonda Rhimes is the first African American woman executive producer and creator of a top 10 primetime televisions series. She didn't give up just because of the competition with so many other television producers and writers. Instead, she pushed on with her why, she conquered, and she produced successful shows like *Grey's Anatomy*, *Scandal*, and *How to Get Away with Murder*.

Women don't work in this field – Look at Ursula Burns, the chair and CEO of Xerox. She was the first black female leader of a Fortune 500 company despite people telling her she had three strikes against her: black, female, and poor. Another woman, Mae Jemison, was the first black female admitted into the astronaut training program and the first black female astronaut in space.

I'm too old - Even older millennials in their late 30s and young Gen Xers face age discrimination just as those much younger or older do. But late bloomers like actor Viola Davis aren't uncommon. After growing up poor with few advantages, she began her acting career in her late 20s and early 30s (late for show business) and worked hard in supporting and minor roles. She won her first award when she was almost 40, and now she's the only African-American to win an Emmy, a Tony, and an Oscar. On top of that, at age 50 she became the first black woman to win the Primetime Emmy Award for Outstanding Lead Actress in a Drama Series: *How to Get Away with Murder*.

You must get rid of all excuses and speak life into yourself. Tell yourself you can do that thing you're working towards despite your circumstances. Even though history may say otherwise, even though your colleague may have been at the job longer than you, even though you may look different from everyone else, even though people may count you out, you have to get rid of those excuses and tell yourself you will succeed.

This no-excuses mantra is applicable while job searching and once you have secured the job. So don't forget it, and don't let that sneaky excuses-thinking seep back in once you land the job. Don't make excuses at work. If you fail to accomplish a task or an assignment, an excuse is not necessary. Get real, instead, and take ownership for your failure and identify ways to fix it. No one wants to hear an excuse; they want to hear a solution or, in some cases, what you need help with to complete a task. Throw out those excuses and replace them with these scriptures or motivational sayings of your own: "I can do all things through Christ which strengthens me" (Philippians 4:13) and "All things work together for good to them that love God, to them who are the called according to his purpose" (Romans 8:28).

Be Knowledgeable and Prepared

You have got to be knowledgeable in your craft. This means you have to become a subject matter expert in your field and the specific area in which you work. If you're a baker, you better know how to measure and combine ingredients, place the dough into pans or baking sheets, and bake for the appropriate amount of time. If you're a cybersecurity expert, you should remain up to date with all of the latest threats and strategies to prevent systems from being compromised.

Your skills and abilities in your specific line of work are the first places ill-intentioned people look for flaws. They will try to discredit you and paint a picture that shows you're not qualified or knowledgeable enough to do your job. But it's your responsibility to do the work required of you independently and accurately. If you lack skills, if you're not actively training, and if you're not knowledgeable in your craft, then it will be difficult to hold your ground.

In one of my former roles, I had the opportunity to present at a roundtable. My topic was a project I was working on to address some of the issues in my organization. Suddenly, out of nowhere, a group of three middle-aged Caucasian men started to ask questions in condescending tones as they expressed their opposing positions. They even made comments that insinuated I was a newbie who didn't know anything.

I immediately felt distressed and under pressure though I think I hid it well, and my first thoughts were, "Oh, my goodness! Why are they talking to me like this!" I couldn't believe it. I was presenting alone and, of course, I had no one who worked with me to back me up. I had to stand up for myself and what I knew was right. But because I was fully knowledgeable about the subject, I was able to address their concerns with confidence and accuracy. I could have easily let their hostility throw me all the way off and back me into a corner, but because I was thoroughly familiar with the topic and body of knowledge surrounding it, I was confident I could match their opposing views.

As stated earlier, no one at that roundtable meeting could have backed me up. I had no one there who could support the work I had done, and you, too, will be on your own with no back up and no one to turn to. There will also be times when colleagues don't or aren't able to extend their promised support and, instead of backing you, they will sit back and watch you drown. You cannot rely on anyone else. Psalms 118:8 says, "It is better to take refuge in the LORD than to trust in man." With that in mind, I am not suggesting that you never trust anyone. Teamwork is needed in many facets of life and the workplace. It requires trust and reliance on those you are working with; however, you must do your part and be knowledgeable in the endeavor or task at hand.

Always make sure you're prepared. Preparation is the key to everything, after all. When you go to meetings, be ready. Remain alert, be on your toes (so to speak), and stay ready – *if you stay ready, you ain't gotta get ready*. Anticipate questions and be able to answer them. When you're knowledgeable in your area, then you can easily be confident in your work and stand up for yourself. And even if you can't answer a particular question, when you're knowledgeable, you're confident enough to clarify the question and promise to get back to them, if needed.

When you're new to a company, it's understandable that you don't know everything and what is expected of you. Many companies have onboarding programs to get you up to par quickly, and once you're clear about your responsibilities, make a point to over-deliver. Plan on reading, studying, or practicing at home or even start work an hour early for a few weeks, if possible. No matter how you do it, get caught up with your colleagues as soon as you're able. And at a minimum, make sure you're meeting all expectations and following procedures.

I also suggest you take advantage of available training, even when it's optional. A lot of companies have educational centers or offer on-site, regularly scheduled training opportunities. Enroll in as many as you can, and seek out additional resources so you're fully prepared for anything that comes your way. And don't worry if something comes up that you're unfamiliar with. It's perfectly okay and expected that you ask questions or request help, clarification, or resources you can use to help bring you up to speed.

Mistakes I have made in the past include not asking questions when I didn't know something and pretending I knew something when I didn't. Those are some of the worst things you can do. Don't be reluctant or ashamed to ask questions; there's a 90% chance that others have asked that same exact same question. Managers and trainers *expect* you to ask questions. Besides, what's the worst that could happen? You get the information you need or you don't. Plus, I've come to find out that nobody knows everything! Even senior employees don't always know the answers, or the question isn't within their specific area of expertise. But asking questions—after you've tried your best to get the answer through your own efforts—also shows you're interested and engaged in the subject matter at hand.

The other thing to never do is pretend you know something when you don't. I know a lot of us can "fake it 'til we make it," but there are some places and situations where that won't work. You can't pretend, for example, to know the exact distance from the earth to the sun if you don't know it.

Besides, it's pretty easy to spot individuals who claim to be well versed in a topic area but really aren't. All it takes is a few questions, and if you're "faking it," then you'll surely be exposed. If you're not familiar with something, just be honest—it's not the end of the world. You were hired for a reason, and most companies understand you won't know everything initially.

Being able to take criticism goes right along with being knowledgeable in your craft and skilled at what you do. Feedback and well-intended criticism provides you with information about yourself you may not know or think is insignificant. I often ask, "What can I do better?" to those individuals who supervise me or are experts in their fields. In order to improve, you must know what areas you lack in and where improvement is needed.

Once you get the job and master your role and responsibilities, don't stop learning. Keep abreast of changes as they occur and new systems, software, procedures, or techniques developing in your area. If you're in technology, you know everything is constantly changing, and since you'll never settle into a routine or get comfortable with your level of mastery, you'll need to be adaptive. Make continuing education courses part of your schedule, and be sure to attend conferences and workshops so you continue to grow. Even in the world of baking, new techniques are constantly developing to enhance the baking experience, save costs, and satisfy customers—think gluten-free, egg-free, milk-free, and vegan products, for starters. So be invested in lifelong learning.

> *"If it's flipping hamburgers at McDonald's, be the best hamburger flipper in the world. Whatever it is you do you have to master your craft."*
> *—Snoop Dogg*

Be Able to Transfer Knowledge

It's not enough to be knowledgeable in your subject area. Another crucial task that goes hand-in-hand with being a subject matter expert is the ability to communicate that knowledge to other individuals or stakeholders. This is where communication skills come in. If you hold a technical position on a multi-disciplinary team, you should be able to communicate technical information to colleagues without a technical background. If you're a subject matter expert and unable to transfer that knowledge, you'll need to learn or improve your communication skills to perform your job effectively.

Improving your communication skills might mean employee training courses if they're offered. I also recommend a thorough self-assessment to learn about your strengths and weaknesses in this area. Self-knowledge and awareness, especially concerning your weaknesses in communication and all other areas, is imperative. When you're aware of the areas in which you need to improve, you can intentionally work to develop and enhance them.

As an example, I can be extremely timid at times, and that's just one area in which I desperately want to improve. I'm not yet sure why or how I can be outgoing and talkative in some situations and don't want to say a word in others, but I acknowledge that this is a flaw I must work on.

Communication, leadership, and behavioral-style assessments, such as the Myers-Briggs personality test, can help. When you know the areas you need to improve in, you can utilize strategies to meet the needs of your environment. I recently took a leadership course where I had the chance to complete the DiSC assessment, which assessed my behavioral style.[13] I learned that I'm an objective thinker, and according to the personal results I received, objective thinkers:

- have advanced critical thinking skills.
- stress the facts when making decisions.
- pursue accuracy in all things.
- desire to work with others, similar to themselves, who are concerned with creating a peaceful atmosphere at work.
- may appear shy to others.
- can be reserved when it comes to articulating feelings.
- try to avoid aggressive individuals.
- while being easy-going and polite, need to be in control of their surroundings.
- are focused on the correct answer and can have difficulty making choices with vague circumstances.
- tend to worry and often get caught up in analysis paralysis.[14]

I think the assessment was spot on. I, too, would call myself an objective thinker. I possess most of the characteristics listed above, some of which I never realized I possessed until I completed the assessment.

The DiSC assessment raised my awareness of areas I need to improve. For example, my discomfort with aggressive people has got to go. I've already encountered aggressive people, as you know by now, and that will never change. My job is to learn how to interact with them and create a win-win situation when possible.

My tendency to be restrained in expressing my feelings can also be a downfall that may prevent me from transferring my knowledge to others. I cannot be shy or timid, as some people perceive me to be and as I know I am on occasion. I must use the appropriate communication skills and strategies to work not only with well-mannered, ambitious people but also with aggressive individuals. Moreover, expressing my feelings on key issues at work based on my knowledge and expertise is also a must.

To help me grow in these areas, I took various courses my organization offered. One of these courses, Handling People with Diplomacy and Tact, taught me strategies to deal with difficult people in addition to various strategies for presenting my ideas. The courses helped a lot—ongoing practice is essential—and I encourage you to seek out classes like this or reach out to mentors who may be able to provide you with guidance and advice.

Be Confidently You

This is one of the most important pieces of advice I have to offer. The message here is to simply be yourself, be confidently you. You must be confident about *you* even when working in an environment with people who are totally different from you. Where they come from may differ, and they may have dissimilar cultural backgrounds and experiences. You should never try to change yourself just to fit in. People have a good eye for noticing when you're not genuine.

I'm from the South, and sometimes I can be really loud and use country slang. Other times I can be very introverted and not in a space where I want to engage in a lot of conversation. At times, especially just out of college, I found myself trying to fit in and talk differently. But that was a mistake, and you should never do that. You are wonderfully made. Nothing about you is a mistake. You should be yourself at all times and people will love you for who you genuinely are. I've since learned at my current job that my team is composed of individuals from all walks of life. By being myself, I've realized I have many things in common with colleagues with whom I assumed I had absolutely nothing in common. I mean, who would have thought that a middle-aged white woman would know who Migos, the rap group, is?

Now in some situations, like meetings attended only by middle-aged white men and me, I can't help but think some of them may be racist and look down on me, a "black girl." Well hey, I had to erase that from my mind and tell myself, "That doesn't matter. I'm here to do my job no matter what anyone thinks of me." And that is what you should be doing. Don't let anyone dim your light. Be confident and unapologetically you.

"Never compromise who you are personally to become who you wish to be professionally." -Janice Bryant Howroyd

Don't Take Things Personally

Now I know there have been several instances where I've discussed how people may feel about me based on their actions towards me. Well, here's the important part: We cannot take their actions personally. Let's revisit the roundtable situation in which the three Caucasian men spoke to me in condescending tones while I presented information about a project that would impact the work they do.

I can't lie. A lot of questions went through my head while they were "going in" on me. "Are these men racist? Do they dislike me? Do they think I can't do my job?" Now that situation was bizarre, I must say, because at all the other roundtables I had attended, these men had never spoken to a presenter in such a hostile or challenging way. I definitely felt like I was being targeted.

After some reflection, I thought, *Well, maybe they didn't have anything against me personally. Maybe they didn't like the implications behind the project outcomes because it would impact them and change their current practices. Maybe they're reluctant to change. Maybe they really have a suggestion or concern that meant a lot to them, and they don't know how to express themselves. Maybe they need a communication skills class. Maybe they're passionate about the subject and that's how they express themselves when they get excited about something.*

It could have very well been about me, my color, or my comparatively young age. Or it could have been about none of those things. But remember, it doesn't matter how people feel about you. It doesn't matter what they say about you. As long as they don't do anything to harm you, threaten your job, or blatantly disrespect or verbally abuse you, then you keep on going about your business. But you have to know that people, no matter their backgrounds, no matter how they feel about you, racist or not, some people will just give you a hard time. We should not take things personally. They very well may have had no issue with me at all.

When we take things personally—when we become upset by or defensive about someone's remarks or actions because we assume they are directed towards us explicitly—it only causes unnecessary anger and frustration. There is no need for frustration because it only impacts us negatively. Don't let what is around you be *in* you. We must understand that we can't control anyone, and we can't change anyone; we can only control our own actions and feelings. Don't let the negative spirits of others fill you up. Protect your peace!

When I first discussed the roundtable, I said that I addressed the concerns of the three men. But I didn't tell you that I addressed their concerns with a sense of humor and a jovial demeanor. I even thanked them for their questions and input. As weird as this may sound, it does you well to respond cheerfully to those who may come at you with an undesirable tone. I know that in the climate we live in today, people are very sensitive to words and actions of others, but we must try our best to not take it to heart.

Now, when that man at my job called me a bitch, I took that personally. A vulgar gesture, clearly and unmistakably directed towards me was personal. Whether he had issues going on outside of work or not, that was unacceptable. *Tell me you'll talk to me later or walk away. Don't call me names.* He was the boss, the leader, a person who sets the tone for appropriate behavior. And because of his position, I, like most would, hold him to a higher standard. I couldn't just let it go because it was clearly directed towards me. This brings me to my next bit of advice: stand up for yourself.

Stand Up for Yourself

If you don't stand up for yourself, no one else will. Now, I'm typically soft-spoken. I guess this totally contradicts what I said earlier when I mentioned I could be loud, but I really am calm and soft-spoken for the most part though being around my family and friends brings out the Southerner in me. But at work, I'm generally calm and composed, and I'm always polite. But I think for some reason, my department lead Joseph took that as a sign of weakness, especially since he had the audacity to call me a word usually considered highly offensive.

Let it be known all over the world that Paige may be gentle and easy-going, but she will stand up for herself EVERY TIME she needs to. Now I could have reacted and "went off" on Joseph immediately. I could have gotten extremely loud and made a scene. I could have let him have it like I've done in the past, but I'm a better person now. I think since I was so shocked, I couldn't say or do anything, and he walked away, which I'm actually glad happened. It gave me a chance to process the event and to come to grips with how I felt. Once I had a chance to calm down and think about the situation, I was ready to stand up for myself and respond.

I urge you to respond and not react. Reacting is typically what you do or how you act immediately after an event. It's short-sighted and impulsive, and it's based on emotions that immediately rise up rather than reasoning. *Responding*, on the other hand, is what you do once you consider the event or situation and think carefully about it. It's deliberate.

Having patience and thinking through your response is imperative. If we react, most of the time we'll end up regretting how we handled the situation. I have learned to be patient and to really think about things from various perspectives before confronting individuals. Fortunately, with the situation with Joseph, I had time to go through all the emotions: disbelief, anger, disappointment, and thoughts of retaliation.

One time, in a situation outside of work, I strained a relationship because of my quick reaction. I was hurt because someone disrespected my mother. In fact, I was enraged. I wanted to protect my mother, but she didn't need my protection. She can hold her own and besides, God is always watching and protecting her, and there was no reason for me to get involved. Had I taken a moment to pause, however, and think things through, a relationship would not have been wounded because of my quick reaction.

In looking back at that, I know if I hadn't learned better ways since then, if I had reacted at work and made a scene for everyone to see or hear, then that would, of course, be outside of my character as they know it. And it would change others' opinions of me and maybe their interactions with me as well. So be deliberate. In responding, make sure you stand up for yourself, but indicate clearly and concisely what the problem is and have examples and support for your case. Be respectful in your response. As Michelle Obama said, "When they go low, we go high."

Don't let people running over you become a habit because, if you let them do it once, they will do it again. They'll keep going and going, seeing how much they can get away with each time. Even with seemingly insignificant things like interruptions at a meeting when you're speaking, don't let that remain unaddressed. Politely but sternly say, "Please let me finish" if someone attempts to cut you off. If you are disrespected, let the individual know that their actions were demeaning and inappropriate. Ask that they not let that type of disrespectful behavior happen again and explain to them that you will not tolerate it.

That said, I strongly suggest that you talk to individuals one-on-one versus "blasting" them in a large group of people. In my situation with Joseph, my immediate supervisor came with me to confront Joseph privately due to the seriousness of what had happened. Plus, I thought it would be best to have a witness and, quite frankly, I had lost any trust I had with him.

Now, if you have been disrespected in a way that rises to the level of harassment of any sort, I suggest you consider speaking with your human resource officer or equal employment office to get assistance with the appropriate steps you should take. Make sure the behavior is addressed appropriately to ensure it doesn't happen again. Many companies have counseling services or assistance programs that provide guidance on issues like these. I sought out our Employee Support Office to learn about the options and support that were available to me in addressing the situation with Joseph. But I still stood up for myself and confronted Joseph face-to-face.

Standing up for yourself is imperative because it ultimately makes the perpetrator aware of their actions and hopefully pushes them to modify their behavior which, in turn, may protect others from similar treatment. In standing up for yourself, you also stand up for others.

"When you react, you are giving away your power. When you respond, you are staying in control of yourself."
– Bob Proctor

Fix Your Face and Control Your Emotions

Yeah, I said it. Fix your face. I can recall hosting a meeting in which I was the organizer and leader. This meeting occurred after the incident with Joseph, and he happened to be one of the attendees. As I was running my meeting and facilitating the conversation to allow for all agenda items to be discussed, I asked if anyone had anything else to add before moving on to another topic, as I usually do. No one had anything to say, so I moved on to the next subject by introducing it verbally.

After speaking on the new topic for a few minutes, Joseph interrupted, wanting to ask about something from the previous topic. This happened multiple times, and I became irritated. Patience is something we all should have with people, and I believe we should be patient with others just as God is patient with us. However, he was working my nerves, partly because it was him. Now I'm the type of person who wears her feelings on her sleeve. If I have an attitude, my face will show it. If I'm daydreaming in the middle of a meeting about the nasty Chinese food I had last night for dinner, my nose is going to be crunched up, and my expression will be one of disgust. So, at some point in the meeting, I became aware of my facial expressions. I had to check myself. I thought, *Paige, fix your face.*

We all need to check ourselves once in a while and even often. Be aware of ourselves. While it may not be your face, it could be your tone of voice or mannerisms. We need to control our emotions when we're in situations with difficult people or people we may not care for. And of course, some things may upset us. We will get angry or we'll get hurt by others, but we cannot let that moment get the best of us and impact our mood or character. Imagine if, after being called out of my name, I got really angry at Joseph and cursed him out loudly in the hallway. I'm pretty sure someone would have seen or heard that. And I'm also pretty sure I would have been the one disciplined and not Joseph. Fortunately, I didn't react. Fortunately, my internal reaction was shock, and I didn't know what to do or say in that moment because it was so unexpected. But during that meeting with Joseph interrupting, I was flat-out annoyed, and I'm pretty sure I rolled my eyes.

"Don't let 'em see you sweat." That's what my father-in-law told me after joking about inviting 50 people to my wedding that my now-husband (his son) didn't even know. Boy, did he have me upset, stressing, face turning red, and eyes rolling. And you know what he told me? "I was just joking with you. You can't let people see you sweat." Although I don't like jokes directed at me, especially when it came to wedding planning, it taught me something: Don't let people see you sweat. Seriously. In other words, don't let people see they're getting to you. Although this wasn't my father-in-law's intent, sometimes people like to do things just to get under your skin. But you have to ignore people like that and focus on your goal. Focus on that meeting. Focus on finishing that project. Focus on you. Let it roll right off your shoulders. Don't take it personally like we discussed earlier.

Because when you do let them see you sweat, they might be getting a kick out of it. It's some kind of enjoyment for them or a bad habit they learned as a kid (probably from being teased themselves), and they'll keep trying to get under your skin, especially if they're prone to bullying. And when they get under your skin, it impacts you. Remember, you can't control anyone else. You can only control your actions. Choose to get irritated or choose to remain calm and go about your business and getting your work done.

So how can you control those emotions? When you feel like you're about to boil over, take a slow, deep breath or two. Fix your face, tell yourself to get it together, and stay calm. One thing that's especially helpful to me is to put things in perspective. Ask yourself, "What's really important here? Is this person important enough to upset me?" Think about the major issues in your life or around the world. There are other things that need this energy stored up inside of you.

Finally, smile. Be polite to the person. Give them the opposite of what they may be expecting from you. I guarantee it will make you feel better. I do it all the time when road rage drivers fuss me out from within their cars, which is a waste of their energy because I can't even hear them. I wave excitedly, smiling, and say hello over and over again.

Learn About Those People You Consider Difficult

If there are certain people who give you a tough time or seem to make everything difficult, you should observe them and try to learn why they behave as they do. It probably has nothing to do with you at all. There can be many reasons people act the way they do based on personality or even their cultural upbringing.

"Jamie," a coworker, was difficult for me to work with, mostly because she was not responsive to emails, and the emails that she did send were brief and lacked sufficient detail for me to complete my tasks. On top of that, when I saw her in the hallway, she was very short with me and seemed standoffish.

One day, a mutual coworker vented to me about her, and I realized in that moment that Jamie wasn't being rude or even trying to annoy me in particular. I wasn't the only person who thought she was tough to work with. My coworker explained that Jamie likes to talk in-person and doesn't do well with emails— *apparently she had been experiencing the same issues*. That made me realize I need to reach out to Jamie and other people in ways that resonate with them. For example, I've learned that some people, baby boomers in particular, prefer face-to-face communication or talking on the phone instead of emails. My fellow colleague who complained to me about Jamie is a millennial just like me, and we're both fine with email and instant messages. But we realized we had to sit down and have a talk with Jamie face-to-face.

If you encounter a situation in which people are challenging to work with, don't get frustrated and judge them. First, try to figure out why they may be acting the way they do. Honestly, the best thing is to talk to them and ask how you can make it easier for them to communicate with you or vice versa.

I'm a newlywed, and in premarital counseling, my husband and I learned that poor communication skills are one of the top reasons that marriages don't last. I think the same applies to work relationships and that communication problems are one of the main reasons for conflict. If communication training is available at your company, take it. It will be well worth your while.

Get You a Mentor

Many of you may have had a mentor before and this is not new to you. Whether it was in high school or college, you may have been paired with someone older than you or someone who has trekked down the same path you're now pursuing. They were there to provide you with information, guidance, and support to help you reach your goals. What you might not realize is that a mentor is still relevant even at work, in your career, and throughout the rest of your life, for that matter.

Having a mentor is extremely important because individuals who are more experienced than you can teach you so many valuable lessons and provide beneficial advice. I'm fairly certain you've heard that saying, "Learn from the mistakes of others." Well, mentors are there to assist you along your journey and help you avoid pitfalls that they may have encountered along theirs. They are there to teach you and give you advice. You should participate in any formal mentorship programs offered in your organization and seek out mentors informally as needed.

It's important to note that you're not limited to only one mentor. You should have a mentor for the various aspects of your life. For example, you may have a mentor for retirement planning and a separate mentor who can provide guidance on the type of work that you do.

One of my mentors also told me you should have a mentor that doesn't look like you. When I heard that I thought, "Wow, I never heard of that!" But it really makes sense to have a mentor of another race or ethnic background because they can provide feedback from a unique perspective. They can offer information that you might not typically get from a person who looks just like you or has a similar background. For that reason, I have and have had mentors who are middle-aged white men and women. Lin, who I referred to earlier, is a middle-aged white man. The middle-aged white woman who has served as my mentor was there for me in the context of being a woman in the workplace and she could provide me with insights about others who looked like her. Keep in mind that I'm not discouraging you from having a mentor that *does* look like you. I believe having a mentor with the same background is crucial because they will have encountered similar issues. I am, however, encouraging you to not limit yourself.

Please note that in the paragraph above, I said that I "have had" mentors. Something else to be aware of is that sometimes mentors may only be yours for a season. Meaning some of your mentors may not be your mentor forever. Some will be lifelong mentors and some will pass knowledge on to you, and then you move on either because you no longer need mentoring in that area or because you need more advanced guidance.

What I want you to get from this is that a diverse group of mentors is invaluable. And they do not always have to be older than you. Some may even be your peers. A mentor is someone who has some type of knowledge that you lack and, therefore, could be someone of the same generation who has experience and knowledge that surpasses yours.

Become Acquainted with Senior Employees and Leadership

Becoming acquainted with senior employees and leadership has many benefits associated with it. The first is that key individuals of the organization who have a lot of influence will become familiar with you. If you can work with them, they also become knowledgeable about the quality of your work. And when they know who you are, they can support you in so many ways such as recommending you for a special task force, supporting you if you need a recommendation of some sort, or serving as a mentor to you. The most important thing you can gain from senior employees and leadership is their knowledge. Learn as much as you can from them.

When I first started in one of the roles I've held, I sought out Lin, an expert who worked on the same type of products as I did. He was the resident expert, and I reached out to him directly, informing him that I was a new employee and that I'd like to talk with him about his work and get advice. Our first conversation consisted of us getting to know each other and learning about each other's backgrounds. He then allowed me to ask questions related to the technical work that we did. Now, he is always there to help me when needed and checks on me if he doesn't hear from me in a while. I was blessed that he was receptive to me and took me on as a mentee. Most leaders generally are accepting of helping others; however, some are too busy or are selective in who they decide to help. Becoming acquainted with Lin also helped me in one particularly interesting situation that I discussed earlier. Lin is that electrical engineer who had my back when my assistant department lead didn't believe in the accuracy of my work. Lin spoke highly of me and indicated that my work was indeed adequate when questioned about it.

Lin is an example of a person who defended me because he knew me and was familiar with my work. If I had never reached out to him, that situation definitely would have played out differently. For one, Lin wouldn't have added me to the email conversation that I was omitted from, and I would have been blind to the fact that my work was being questioned without my awareness. If Lin was unfamiliar with me and my work, then his response might have been different altogether and not as supportive as it was.

So, don't be afraid to get out there and introduce yourself to those in leadership roles or those who have been with the organization for many years. Attend "town hall" meetings or meetings in which these individuals may be the host or the presenter. Go speak to them, introduce yourself, and ask questions. This is how relationships form and the door to mentorship opens.

Do you feel intimidated by higher-ups or just feel too shy to approach them? It wasn't easy for me, but you have to remember that they are people just like you. They probably have stood in your same shoes before. So speak to them if you see them in passing. I suggest before approaching a senior-level employee or leader, prepare a few questions in advance that you'd like to ask them. But don't begin with the questions. Introduce yourself and let them know who you are. Then let them know that you are familiar with their work, mentioning specific examples, and that you would love to have a chance to sit down with them for a conversation. You could then mention your questions or specific interests. This should open the door for future discussions. And if you don't have the privilege of seeing them in passing, sending an email in the same manner should suffice. However, I caution you that sometimes emails do get lost when reaching out to leaders who are busy with other priorities, so if you see them in person, don't let that opportunity to introduce yourself pass you by.

Find a Support Network or Organization

"As iron sharpens iron, so one man sharpens another."
-Proverbs 27:17 (AMP)

I am not the only woman who has encountered issues in the workplace like those I've been describing throughout this book. I know because I've seen some of my friends and family on social media complaining about many of the same issues that I've faced. I've seen women in entertainment and participants of the #MeToo and #TimesUp movements talk about the treatment that they've received. With that in mind, it's likely there are women or other people like you in your organization who are going through the same types of things that you are going through. We don't have to deal with these things alone. We can band together to support each other.

Why not seek out a network of women or an organization designed for mutual support? There may be organizations already formed which you can join or you may be able to form a group yourself. At my first job, I became a member of a professional chapter of the National Society of Black Engineers (NSBE). This organization, along with others like it, support women and underrepresented minorities who encounter some of the same issues. While these organizations have their own individual goals, such as outreach into the community, they also have programs to help support their members and the difficulties they may encounter in the workplace.

I found NSBE to be a safe haven. This was a group I could

spend time with and talk with about issues we encountered in the workplace. I was able to connect with individuals who had been at their jobs for years, and they were able to provide insight to the newer employees like me. When times get tough, encouragement from those who believe in you is really uplifting. That is what I found in NSBE, and I encourage you to find a similar group. It doesn't have to be something formal. It can just consist of you and a few other colleagues you trust or even neighbors or residents of your town or city who work in the same field. I occasionally go to lunch with two trusted coworkers, and we talk a lot about the challenges we face. We look out for each other and support each other through tough times.

You should also find support and activities outside of work, as well, to develop and maintain a work-life balance. Attending church and volunteering in some way are the top things on my list of activities outside of work. I used to lead the youth dance ministry which I enjoyed tremendously. I have also spent time volunteering at "The Village." The Village is a community center for students to receive mentoring and educational opportunities like tutoring. There I met families who welcomed me as their own and even people who have become lifelong friends. Communities of support like these are critical to your overall well-being and can also help you in your career.

Embrace Diversity

Today within many companies, diverse groups of people who come from many different backgrounds work together. We should take the opportunity to learn about those who are different from us. We should embrace diversity, embrace other cultures, and learn more about others, their traditions, and how they may impact the way people act and the things they do. When we understand what makes people tick, so to speak, we can be sensitive to them and learn how to interact and communicate with them effectively.

Despite the fact that there are some racist people in the workforce, there are also people who are not racist and who believe in equality no matter the race, ethnicity, gender, or background of a person. There are good people out there. We should be extremely mindful not to be unconsciously judgmental. I admit that I have unintentionally judged individuals based on their background or how they look. And these preconceived notions were based on my experiences growing up. However, I had to do a self-check. These judgmental thoughts are the same types of thoughts that grow into the type of behavior and treatment that I advocate against. Oh, if we lived in a world where we didn't look at the exterior of people but learned about what they possess on the inside, the world would be a much better place. So, check yourself. Never judge someone by their appearance because that is not even half of their story.

Embrace diversity. Our nation is a melting pot of people from all over the world. Together we can do so much.

Remember Who and Whose You Are

In all the trials that you face, remember who you are. I often tell myself that I am strong, smart, courageous, and capable. I am a conqueror. I am who God says I am, and God says that I am "fearfully and wonderfully made" (Psalms 139:14). God says that I am the "head and not the tail" (Deuteronomy 28:13). I am above and not beneath. I have no reason to fear or to let people discourage me or run me away because all things will work out for my good according to His works. And I know the plans that he has for me—plans to help me prosper and not let me be harmed.

You too are strong and courageous. You are a conqueror and you can do all things. Never forget that and never let anyone else tell you otherwise. Never change or compromise your values and morals. Be boldly you!

I want you to not only remember who you are but also *whose* you are. Earlier in this book, I mentioned how the president can be equated to the boss of the country. Well, while the president may run the nation we live in and while your supervisor may instruct you on what to do, you are not theirs. You do not belong to them. We are all children of God. God is the only one we have to answer to and through Him we can do anything. It doesn't matter if it's something that's never been done before or something that has never been done by a person like you. If God put that goal, that dream, that job, or whatever it is you're seeking in your heart, then nothing can take it away from you. If He leads you to it, He will certainly guide you through it. So, don't rely too much on people, and don't let people and their opinions put a limit on you and what you can achieve. For you belong to an all-powerful God who's got your back!

"I'm a strong black woman and I cannot be intimidated, I cannot be undermined .... Don't allow these...dishonorable people to intimidate you or scare you, be who you are, do what you do... We also know that when a woman stands up and speaks truth to power, that there will be attempts to put her down. And so I am not going to be put down, I'm not going to go anywhere, I'm going to stay..."
—*Maxine Waters*

Now What?

I imagine you've committed to becoming a conqueror if you've made it this far. You've read about my experiences, and you have taken the time to go through my suggestions for thriving in environments where you may encounter difficulties. So now what? Well, you can go ahead and put my recommendations to the test:

- Get rid of your excuses
- Master your craft
- Be able to share your knowledge
- Be unapologetically and confidently you
- Don't take things personally
- Stand up for yourself
- Fix that face, girl, and grab ahold of those emotions
- Observe and learn about those you work with
- Get you a mentor
- Connect with experienced colleagues and leaders
- Find a support system
- Embrace diversity
- Remember who you are and who you belong to

You may find other strategies not discussed that can help you in your circumstances. If something works for you, embrace it! My recommendations are practices that have worked for me, and I'm sure there are others that may be beneficial to you.

The key message here is that encountering trials and situations in your career is inevitable, and you can make it through them. They are growth opportunities and even allow you to help others. So, once you get a grasp on things and are conquering your workplace or any other space, assist those who may be encountering some of the same challenges. Here are some things you can do to help.

Tell Your Story

What prompted me to write this book came after the feedback I received after making a couple of posts on social media about challenges in the workplace. Several people commented on my statuses and indicated that they, too, had encountered similar situations. I realized I was not the only one with these types of experiences and that maybe I could help others and serve as support for them.

The trials we have gone through turn out to be testimonies that can give others encouragement to keep pushing forward. So, don't be shy or try to hide your story. It can help others who might desperately need advice or assistance and show people that they're not alone, and that they too can be a conqueror.

Be a Mentor to Others

There is a need for mentors and role models to support young women and college students as they navigate through racism, sexism, and microaggressions in a professional work environment. I discussed mentoring earlier from the viewpoint of finding someone who could serve as a source of guidance and knowledge to you. Now I am reversing the roles and suggesting that you fulfill the role of mentor. You have gone through challenges and come out on top, now it's time for you to share your knowledge to help others just like you in need.

Initiate Change

If you have realized that, institutionally, things are not fair to everyone, be the person who spearheads change and advocates for equality. By helping to break down systematic processes or eliminating inappropriate behavior and mistreatment practices in the workplace, you can help create a new environment for those coming up behind you.

Life After "The Incident"

So, you may be wondering, what was life like after the incident that occurred with my department lead, the man who called me a bitch? Well, I can tell you that I didn't quit. I didn't run away. I can also tell you that after that incident, his behavior towards me changed drastically. It was actually a bit odd if only because he seemed to have flipped a switch. He was extremely nice to me. He even allowed me to take advantage of opportunities not traditionally allowed. The change in behavior could be because he sincerely felt bad for what he said, and he was genuinely trying to change. Or it could be he was terrified I'd inform someone other than my supervisor about what he did and additional consequences that might come his way. But no matter the reason, he decided to change his behavior. I cannot speak for his heart, but from the outside, he appears to have changed.

This situation did not take me out. Yes, it knocked me down briefly, but I got up. I don't stay down. I can't stay down. I didn't let this change the way I felt about my job or the work because I really enjoyed the organization. I was not going to let one unpleasant experience spoil everything.

Many people may fear that after a negative experience with someone from management, they may be blackballed or ostracized. Well, I definitely didn't worry about that because I knew that my work would speak for me. My character and how I treat others spoke for me, and no person can tear down what I built. My immediate supervisor was very supportive, as mentioned earlier. I received the highest ratings on my yearly performance assessments with that particular organization, and I was recognized and received awards based on my performance. All of these accolades had to receive departmental sign-off by the one who had disrespected me. So, no, I didn't let anyone stop me from doing something I enjoy. I will never do that.

There are still challenges that I may encounter at work. Shoot, I encounter some of the same challenges in other areas of my life. But I keep going. This world that we live in is full of issues. There will always be problems blocking our way. The devil will always try to knock us down, and we have to deal with it. We have to keep moving forward.

I still need more practice with some of the tips I have shared—repetition of new thinking or behavior until it's fully integrated into our habits is how we learn. Not taking things personally and fixing my face are among the top things to improve on my list.

I also remind myself that situations like this will happen again. It's inevitable based on the current state of our country and the world, and even if we made progress in the last few years, racism, sexism, and any -ism you can imagine won't disappear overnight. So while always hoping for the best, I am prepared to conquer all challenges I may face in the workplace and every aspect of my life.

Closing

Judgment is inevitable. We will be judged based on our looks, our age, the way we talk, and many other aspects of ourselves we have little or no control over. While people are entitled to their private opinions, they should not let their views lead to mistreatment or unfairness towards others. But we all know many don't agree with that sentiment, and with that in mind, you must be prepared to stand up for yourself when you realize you're being mistreated.

I want to reiterate that. Stand up for yourself. Advocate for yourself. If you do not advocate for yourself, no one else will. You have a voice, an opinion, talent, and skills that matter. Don't you dare retreat to a corner when confronted with challenges. Approach them head-on, instead.

Remember, always, you are strong. You are courageous. You are a conqueror!

Your Personal Why

About the Author

 Hello! I am Paige Brown, a native of Ahoskie, North Carolina and a graduate of North Carolina Agricultural & Technical State University. Aggie Pride! I am an electrical engineer by trade but a passionate STEM education advocate and educator (mostly in informal learning settings) at heart. As an electrical engineer, I have been exposed to technical settings that have not always been inclusive of people of color. To escape those harsh environments, I began devoting my time to educating and exposing students to the world of STEM. I enjoy teaching students in any setting, classroom and beyond, about the field of engineering and how to maximize their success throughout their educational career. Volunteering with organizations such as the National Society of Black Engineers, Alpha Kappa Alpha Sorority, Inc., and small-scale community efforts in my hometown allowed my passion for STEM education to grow. This zeal for working with students led me to pursue my Ph.D. in Engineering Education, where my current research interests involve understanding the experiences of black women in the engineering workforce (fueled by my own personal experiences) and K-12 engineering education of underrepresented minorities. I plan to continue my work and strive for a greater impact in the field of engineering to provide a more inclusive environment for women of color and minorities.

Notes

[1] "Selected Supreme Court Decisions." U.S. Equal Employment Opportunity Commission. Accessed October 1, 2018. https://www.eeoc.gov/eeoc/history/35th/thelaw/supreme_court.html.

[2] Slaton, Amy E. *Race, Rigor, and Selectivity in U.S. Engineering: The History of an Occupational Color Line.* Cambridge: Harvard University Press, 2010.

[3] Leonhardt, David, and Ian Prasad Philbrick. "Donald Trump's Racism: The Definitive List." The New York Times. January 15, 2018. Accessed May 18, 2018. http://www.nytimes.com/interactive/2018/01/15/opinion/leonhardt-trump-racist.html.

[4] Riechmann, Deb. "Trump Hosts Young Blacks, Marvels at Kanye's Impact." The Washington Post. October 26, 2018. Accessed October 27, 2018. https://www.washingtonpost.com/politics/trump-hosts-young-black-conservative-leaders-at-white-house/2018/10/26/a6bd9d94-d950-11e8-8384-bcc5492fef49_story.html?utm_term=.7f33a92c4d8b.

[5] Hayes, Christal. "Here Are 10 times President Trump's Comments Have Been Called Racist." USA Today. August 15, 2018. Accessed August 20, 2018. https://www.usatoday.com/story/news/politics/onpolitics/2018/08/14/times-president-trump-comments-called-racist/985438002/.

[6] "Bill of Rights." Bill of Rights Institute. Accessed June 1, 2018. https://billofrightsinstitute.org/founding-documents/bill-of-rights/.

[7] Bill of Rights.

[8] Swanson, Kelly. "Trump Tells Cops They Should Rough People up More during Arrests." Vox. July 28, 2017. Accessed August 20, 2018. https://www.vox.com/policy-and-politics/2017/7/28/16059536/trump-cops-speech-gang-violence-long-island.

[9] Quillian, Lincoln, Devah Pager, Ole Hexel, and Arnfinn H. Midtbøen. "Meta-analysis of Field Experiments Shows No Change in Racial Discrimination in Hiring over Time." *Proceedings of the National Academy of Sciences* 114, no. 41 (2017): 10870-0875. doi:10.1073/pnas.1706255114.

[10] Rincon, Roberta M., and Nicole Yates. "Women of Color in the Engineering Workplace: Early Career Aspirations, Challenges, and Success Strategies." National Society of Black Engineers. 2018. Accessed August 20, 2018. www.nsbe.org/getmedia/b01e0f12-9378-46b0-ad4d-a0f513b947a5/Women-of-Color-Research-2018.aspx.

[11] Rincon and Yates.

[12] Williams, David R. "How Racism Makes Us Sick." TED: Ideas worth Spreading. Accessed October 26, 2018. https://www.ted.com/talks/david_r_williams_how_racism_makes_us_sick?language=en.

[13] "DiSC Profile - What Is DiSC®? The DiSC Personality Profile Explained." DiSCProfile.com. Accessed January 05, 2018. https://www.discprofile.com/what-is-disc/overview/.

[14] DiSC Profile.